DA

THE MYSTERY OF "TALKING" ANIMALS

by
Lila Walz

Illustrated by
Gerald Smith

This book is distributed by Silver Burdett Company, Morristown, New Jersey 07960.

Library of Congress Number: 79-17127

Art and Photo Credits

Cover illustration by Gerald Smith

Cover illustration and illustrations on pages 11, 29, 31, 36, and 47, courtesy of Coronet Instructional Media, a division of Esquire, Inc.
Photo on page 7, Yerkes Regional Primate Research Center of Emory University
Photos on pages 9, 41, 43, and 44, S. Olan.
Photos on pages 17, 21, and 38, Bruce Coleman, Inc.
Photo on page 48, Beatrice Gardner.
Every effort has been made to trace the ownership of all copyrighted material in this book and to obtain permission for its use.

Library of Congress Cataloging in Publication Data

Walz, Lila
The mystery of "talking" animals.

SUMMARY: Describes the various ways animals, principally chimpanzees and dolphins, are being taught to communicate with human beings.
1. Animal communication — Juvenile literature. 2. Human-animal communication — Juvenile literature. [1. Animal communication. 2. Human-animal communication] I. Title.
QL776.W35 599'.05'9 79-17127
ISBN 0-89547-077-2

Manufactured in the United States of America
ISBN 0-89547-077-2

Contents

Chapter 1

The Keyboard and the Strange Black Box

Lana races over to the panel of buttons. Her eyes dart across the pictures that cover the buttons. She seems to be looking for only one. Suddenly she finds it. She pushes the button. Rock music fills the room. This is the kind of music Lana likes. She claps her hands to the heavy beat of the bass guitar.

Now Lana begins to dance. Her arms wave about. Her feet step in time with the music. Her whole body swings back and forth as her favorite rock songs fill the room. This is not what you would call the best dancing you have ever seen. But she *is* having fun.

As Lana grows tired of the music she pushes the button again. The tape machine stops. The room is quiet once more. But it is *too* quiet! Maybe a movie will be a nice change of pace. Lana thinks for a moment before she decides what film she would like to see. Then at the touch of her finger a *Bugs Bunny* cartoon flashes onto a white screen in front of her. Lana is happy with her choice. Her lips break into a wide grin.

When the movie ends, the room is still again. Lana feels lonely. She looks about. She can eat if she wants. She can watch another movie or listen to some more music. But Lana wants to do none of these things. She isn't bored. Lana is simply lonely. She misses her friend. It is hard to spend all day with someone and then be left alone in the evening. And it probably does not help Lana a bit that she is taking part in an important scientific experiment.

Nor does it seem to make a difference that Lana is not a human being. She is a *chimpanzee*. But she is still lonely.

Perhaps Lana does not know just how important she is to the experiment. Scientists are trying to teach her to "talk." No one expects that the chimp will actually say words we can understand. But Lana is learning some new ways to tell human beings exactly what she is thinking.

The lonely chimp peers through the glass walls of her room. But there is no one to "talk" to. It is evening. Her teacher and all the others have gone home.

So Lana returns to the panel of large buttons. They

look like very large typewriter keys. Covering each key is a picture. Each picture has a meaning. A picture can stand for an object, a word, or an idea.

Can a chimpanzee really "read" these pictures? Can Lana actually use this picture language to typewrite messages to humans? The answer is that Lana *must* read and write. She must use the keys to name different objects and to get food and other things she wants. If Lana feels hungry, she must push the button with the picture that means "food." That is the only way she can get herself a meal.

Lana does most of her "typing" when her human friend is with her. Her friend, the scientist who taught her how to type, spends a lot of time with her. It is important to measure how well Lana knows what the pictures mean and how quickly she can learn the meaning of new pictures. But does this mean that Lana is really learning to "talk"? Perhaps what Lana does next will help you answer this question.

The lonely chimp looks at the typewriter panel for a while. She appears to be deep in thought. She studies the pictures. Suddenly she starts pushing the big buttons, one after another. This time she is not just calling for another movie or song. Can this chimpanzee be typing a message to someone? A machine in the next room changes the pictures on the buttons into

Lana can listen to music or watch a movie just by touching the right button on her keyboard.

words. Lana stands back. She waits for her friend to come to the window. But nobody comes. By now Lana is tired, and she goes to sleep.

The next morning Lana's teacher arrives and reads the message typed by the chimpanzee:

PLEASE MACHINE. COME PLAY WITH ME.

Lana lives in a laboratory where a group of scientists study her ability to think and to use language. At the same time another research team is doing something quite different to learn more about animal "talk."

Mamie swims through the cool blue water. Mamie seems to be feeling playful today. The day is clear and the sun warms her back as she swims. She dives all the way to the bottom of the pool. In a moment she races to the surface again. As she does, she kicks up a shower of water that splashes everyone sitting around the pool. Then she leaps away as everyone splashes water back at her. It's a water fight — between Mamie, a dolphin, and the humans who are watching her play. Mamie loves the action. She is a natural clown and splashing is her favorite joke on people.

But it looks like a joke may have been played on Mamie at the same time. She dives underwater and swims to the wall at the farthest end of the pool. There she finds something she has never seen before. Someone has placed a strange black box in the water. It seems harmless. The curious dolphin swims up for a closer look. There has never been anything like this in the pool before. What can it be? Mamie feels the box with her snout. She swims around near the box and makes a few sounds into it.

Seconds later Mamie gets quite a surprise. She hears a sound coming back to her through the box. Or rather, she hears sounds and they are just like the ones she just made. Before long Mamie is deep in conversation with the black box. It seems to make the same high-pitched dolphin beeps and quick clicking sounds that she makes.

In a pool close to Mamie's swims Willie — another dolphin. Willie, too, hears sounds coming from a black box he has never seen before. When he hears the sounds of a dolphin coming to him from the box, Willie starts to make sounds back at the box. And so it is that two dolphins that have never met are able to talk with each other. From one pool to another, the dolphins carry on beeping, clicking telephone conversations.

Mamie and Willie, like Lana, the chimpanzee, are part of an important experiment. Scientists know that dolphins are probably the smartest of the water animals. Like humans, dolphins are mammals. And like humans, they make many different sounds and movements that seem to make sense to other dolphins. Scientists are now trying to find out if there is a dolphin "language." Do dolphins like Mamie and Willie really "talk" to each other?

To find out, the scientists put small black boxes, called *hydrophones*, into the two pools where Mamie

Are the dolphin's beeps and high-pitched clicking sounds really a language? Scientists all over the world are trying to find out.

and Willie live. The test seemed to work! The dolphins struck up a "conversation" on the hydrophones just like two humans talking on the telephone. They even continued their chat after their line had been disconnected for a while — just as humans would.

But questions still need to be answered. Were Mamie and Willie really "talking"? Is Lana's picture typing really a language? These animals don't use human words, but they can make humans understand what they want and need. How do they do it? What is their "talk" all about?

Animal "talk" is one of nature's greatest mysteries. But humans have already discovered some exciting clues . . . clues that are helping us break the codes animals use to get in touch with each other.

These clues to animal language come from the work scientists are doing all over the world.

The stories in this book are based on just a few of these exciting studies.

Chapter 2

A Journey to the Wild

Dr. James Walker pulled open the tent flap. The early morning air was cool and still. But the blazing red sun just showing over the horizon told Walker what to expect. In a few hours it would be almost too hot to move. The mists, rising like steam from the damp earth, had already begun to burn away.

By now Dr. Walker was used to the heat and the daily rains. He and his two assistants, Ralph Mandell and Agnes Corelli, had come to Tanzania three months ago. The burning sun and the thick green foliage of the African rain forest were beginning to feel like home. Indeed, their forest camp *was* home. It would be for quite a while. The many different animals and birds were no longer strange or frightening. The group was learning to share the jungle quite peacefully with their animal neighbors.

Ralph, an early riser, poured coffee for the group. Then he returned to the tape recorder he had been repairing. Agnes was just coming back with a bucket of water. A quick morning wash, a bit of breakfast, and the work day would begin.

"I wonder where the rest of the family is this morning," said Agnes. "Do you think their alarm clock is broken?"

Dr. Walker laughed. "Maybe they're having trouble finding breakfast. You know how Big Daddy loves to eat. He won't be back until he finds his favorite berries."

"When they get here, we'll be ready. If they chatter as much as they did yesterday, we'll be busy for a long time," said Ralph. He smiled as he snapped a new tape into the recorder. "There, it's as good as new. Now let's hope our friends give us a good recording."

These scientists have come to the African forest to study chimpanzees. They want to know more about the way chimps talk with each other. Armed with tape recorders, they catch every sound the chimps make. They use movie cameras to film the actions that go with the sounds. When film and tape are played at the same time, movements and sounds can be put together. If each time a chimp makes a certain sound another chimp acts a certain way, perhaps the

scientists will learn what the sound means. If they can learn the meaning of enough sounds, this team could teach the human world a new language — the language of chimpanzees.

Suddenly there is a noise in the thick brush around the camp. Looking up, the scientists see the trees shake. Their chimp family is coming home from a search for breakfast. Clutching berry vines, the four chimps amble into the clearing. The animals hardly notice that Agnes has turned on the movie camera. The chimps and the humans are so used to one another they *do* seem like a family.

Walker's group has given each chimp a name. "Big Daddy" is a full-grown male chimp. He is the largest of the group. He is also the leader of the group. Big Daddy helps "Aunt Mary," an adult female chimp, look after "Pete" and "Lulu," the two babies of the family.

Lulu bounces along behind Aunt Mary. She is trying to take an extra bunch of berries, but Aunt Mary shoos her away. Aunt Mary settles down to eat in a cool spot near the table where Dr. Walker sits taking notes. Lulu has already forgotten about the berry vines. She picks some grass from the ground near Dr. Walker's feet. Every now and then she chews some grass and looks up at the scientist with a grin that seems to say, "Mmm, very tasty!"

In the wild, chimpanzees live in groups. They are, in many ways, like human families.

Big Daddy has found his favorite dining spot. He is sitting on a fallen log at the edge of the camp. He watches the family finish their breakfast of grass and berries. The chimps are making soft, grunting sounds. Walker and the others know this means they are happy. Lulu has already finished her dessert of fresh grass. Now she wants Aunt Mary to play with her. She makes smacking noises with her lips and chatters with her teeth. She calls out "ah-ah-ah" in a high-pitched voice.

But Aunt Mary ignores the mischievous baby. She just keeps eating berries. Between bites she looks up to mumble something to Big Daddy. And Big Daddy grunts back as if to say, "Not a bad meal at all." This might be breakfast in any human family.

Suddenly Agnes stops her camera. Something is wrong. "Where's Pete?" she asks Dr. Walker. "It's not like him to miss a meal."

But at that moment there is a rustling in the brush. Pete dashes into the clearing. Big Daddy greets Pete with a soft "hoo-hoo." But Pete is too excited to reply. He rushes wildly about in a circle, looking over his shoulder. He opens his mouth wide and draws back his lips to show his large teeth. Dr. Walker, Ralph, and Agnes know what Pete is trying to say: "Help! I'm scared! Something's after me!"

Big Daddy hops off his fallen log and dashes over to Pete. Following the young chimp in his mad dance of terror, Big Daddy keeps tapping Pete softly on the back. This is the big chimp's way of saying, "Hey, take it easy! There's nothing to worry about. I'm here, and I'll protect you." And to show that he means it, Big Daddy lumbers off into the part of the forest where Pete had first appeared.

Pete still seems very frightened. But Big Daddy's "words" appear to have calmed him. He looks up when Aunt Mary pats the tree limb on which she is sitting. Pete accepts Aunt Mary's invitation. He leaps up to sit next to her. She quiets him by gently picking through and cleaning the hair on his back and head. She makes soft sounds to comfort Pete. She purses her lips and sometimes sticks out her tongue.

Now Pete seems fully calm again. He holds out his hand, hungry for the breakfast he never had. Aunt Mary puts some berries in Pete's hand. They disappear in one swallow.

Suddenly several loud barks shatter the quiet. It's Big Daddy, calling from the forest. "Be careful! There's danger!" Whatever it was that scared Pete now seems to be scaring the big chimp as well.

Big Daddy leaps into the clearing as if shot from a

cannon. Two more sharp barks: "We'd better get out of here fast!" Then he rushes to the far side of the clearing. He seems not even to see his human friends just a few feet away. He looks back once, making movements and sounds that mean, "Follow me . . . . Quick!"

Not a moment too soon, the four chimps disappear into the forest. Now the scientists see for the first time what was so frightening to the chimps. There, at the edge of their camp, is a silent, stalking, black-maned lion!

The powerful lion stops and sniffs the air. Its fierce, cold eyes scan the clearing. Then its tail begins to swing quickly from side to side. But Dr. Walker and his group are hardly worried. They know that lions don't like to be around people. The beast in the clearing is probably much more uneasy than they are. And sure enough, the lion turns and leaps away as fast as it appeared.

"Well!" says Ralph, switching off the tape recorder. "The chimps really gave us something to study today. This is the first time we have seen them sense real danger. I'll say one thing for them. They certainly take good care of each other."

Agnes agreed. "Humans couldn't have warned each other any more quickly!"

Chimps are able to warn each other when danger is near. But how much do these warning calls really say?

But all three scientists found themselves wondering about the same questions. Did Big Daddy bark just to make a warning *noise*? Or did the barks tell his family more? Was he saying, *"There's a big lion back here"*?

Did the chimps hear from Big Daddy only that there was danger? Or did he also tell them *what* the danger was? Do animals like the chimpanzees have a natural "language"? Is it like our own language — a system of words in a code others can understand? Will it ever be possible for chimps to understand *humans* through some "language" of sounds and movements?

Scientists like Dr. Walker are asking such questions, and at least one more about the animals they study: Can an ape, already so much like a human, learn to *talk* — form understandable words — like a human?

Chapter 3

Conversations with a Gorilla

The park near Koko's home has lots of beautiful flowers. Koko loves to roll and play near the bright flower beds. And though she is not supposed to, Koko often leaves the park with a bunch of flowers she has picked.

Yes, Koko loves going to the park. And so does Mike, Koko's young friend. They both get a great kick out of rolling in the grass or playing Frisbee with Penny, their teacher. Koko and Mike are gorillas. Penny Patterson is a psychologist who is trying to teach the young gorillas to use the language of humans.

On a sunny Tuesday afternoon Koko decided to do some exploring in the park. Taking Mike by the hand, she walked along the paths through the gardens. That's when she saw them — dozens of bright blue flowers she had not seen before. Blue is Koko's favorite color. She couldn't resist. Making sure Penny couldn't see, Koko began to pull at the flowers. She grabbed great handfuls, tearing them out of the ground roots and all. Koko grinned proudly. She had put together a beautiful bunch of flowers.

Mike clapped his hands. He wanted some flowers too. But Koko had picked them all. He'd have to take some from Koko — if Koko would share them with him. She wouldn't. Perhaps Koko knew that Mike would want to show them to Penny. That would get them *both* into trouble. Mike was younger than Koko. He had never seen how angry Penny got when Koko picked flowers.

Suddenly Mike began to tickle Koko. At the same time he reached for the flowers in her hands. Several flowers fell to the ground, and Mike swooped them up. He dashed off to show them to Penny, who was reading under a nearby tree. Koko was angry. She glared at Mike. But that didn't seem to bother the young male gorilla very much.

Suddenly Koko placed her open hand flat against her forehead. She made this sign three times. It meant, "I am angry at you. You are bad."

GSmith

Now Koko sits in a corner of the house trailer where she and Mike live. She is facing the wall. Penny is nearby, but she doesn't say a word. Koko is being punished for pulling up the flowers.

Penny has already explained things to the flower-picking gorilla. "I am not just angry about the flowers," she has told Koko. "I am unhappy about the way you talked back to me today." Koko hangs her head, unable to look her teacher in the eye. The usually playful gorilla knows she has done something even worse than picking some flowers in the park.

"You dirty bad," Koko had said when Penny scolded her about the flowers. "Rotten nut you." Koko was *really* mad, and she wanted Penny to know it. But the human teacher soon had had enough of Koko's insults.

Now the gorilla and her teacher have stopped talking to each other, just as any friends might after an argument. Koko stands quietly in the corner, hoping her teacher will give her a hug and say, "O.K., I forgive you." If that happens quickly enough and the sun is still up, Koko can go back to the park this afternoon. *With a little luck, she might even pick some more flowers!*

Penny Patterson is not really too angry at her gorilla student. The teacher may not have liked what the angry gorilla had to say to her this afternoon. But as a teacher, she is really quite proud. After all, Koko had something to say to a human. And she knew how to say it.

Penny Patterson is a researcher who is studying the ability of apes to learn a human language. She has found a very bright pupil in this gorilla she calls Koko. But Patterson is not the first scientist to try to teach apes to "talk." Much of what she already knows about animal language came from the earlier work of others. They learned long ago that apes, such as gorillas and chimpanzees, cannot make different spoken words as humans do. The ape's mouth, voice box, and vocal cords are quite different from ours.

Following the example of earlier scientists, Penny Patterson is communicating with Koko and Mike through another kind of human language. It is called *American Sign Language*, or Ameslan. American Sign Language is made up of many different hand motions. Each movement of the hands stands for a word or idea. Through sign language a person can say anything he or she wants to without making a single sound. Once used only by people who could not hear or speak, today sign language is being used by people who want to talk with animals.

Before trying to teach sign language to Koko, Penny Patterson studied the work of Allen and Beatrice Gardner. The Gardners taught a chimpanzee named Washoe to "talk" using sign language.

Washoe learned one hand sign at a time. Over and over, the Gardners taught her the signs for different objects. Then they moved to signs for actions like "give," "take," and "bring," and for the words "you" and "me." After ten months Washoe began to understand that these word signs could be joined to make sentences.

The Gardners worked hard and long with Washoe. It was difficult to know if the chimp really was learning to use a human language. Then one day they had their answer. Washoe was watching her trainer enjoying a candy bar. Washoe wanted some candy too. The trainer knew what the unhappy chimp wanted, but she decided that Washoe was going to have to ask for it. Washoe walked back and forth across the floor. The chimp seemed to be thinking through a big problem. Then suddenly Washoe stopped. She turned and ran up to the trainer, quickly making signs with her hands and fingers. The delighted trainer watched Washoe say something completely on her own: "Gimme sweet ... gimme sweet ... gimme sweet."

"Gimme sweet" was an important event for every scientist in the world then working with apes. Just a couple of simple words, but they were a beginning. Washoe was only a little over one-and-a-half years old. That was just about the age when most human children also begin to put simple words together. Soon Washoe was signing more short sentences: "Open key food"

The Gardners taught Washoe a human sign language. The only way she could get a reward — some prize she wanted — was to ask for it with the right sign words.

("Please open the locked refrigerator — I want to eat!") and "You tickle me" ("Please play with me.").

Like a small human child, Washoe showed her teachers that she had a mind of her own. She certainly knew what she wanted. And when she didn't know the right word for something, she'd just make one up. But could Washoe think for herself in more difficult ways? Could she, for example, use word signs she already knew to name something she *didn't* know? To find out, her trainer gave her a piece of watermelon. There was no word in Washoe's vocabulary for the sweet watermelon fruit she liked so much. That didn't stop Washoe! Right away she made the signs for "water ... fruit" and "drink ... fruit."

People who heard about the young chimpanzee's use of sign language were amazed. But Washoe's made-up words were more than amazing. They were very important clues to the scientists trying to teach animals to "talk." Washoe was using Ameslan (American Sign Language) signs that she had been *taught*. But she was also putting them together in ways she had *never* been taught. A chimpanzee was using human language in the same way humans do!

Penny Patterson read every word she could find about the Gardners and their work with the "talking" chimp. She came to listen to the Gardners speak about their exciting new work with Washoe. The more she read and the more she heard, the more questions she had. Patterson soon found herself wondering if a baby gorilla she had seen at the San Francisco zoo could also learn American Sign Language.

Most scientists who had studied apes believed that gorillas were not as bright as chimpanzees. If that were true, gorillas probably could not learn a language as chimpanzees had. But Patterson did not believe this was true. She decided to try teaching a gorilla to "talk."

Her student would be Koko — the ape she had met at the zoo.

Patterson started teaching Koko to talk just as the Gardners had started with Washoe. She would make the same hand signs over and over again until Koko could make them too. She would place an object, such as a cup, in front of Koko. Then she would "mold" the gorilla's hand and fingers into the sign for "cup." At first Koko would not cooperate. She tried to bite her teacher every time Penny tried to mold the gorilla's

hands into a sign. Patterson was worried. But she wouldn't give up on Koko.

Soon the teacher's patience paid off. Koko turned out to be a bright and willing student. She seemed to like being able to "talk" with her teacher. How good a student can a gorilla become? Maybe Penny Patterson's gorilla can give us the answer. Today Koko has a vocabulary of over 375 signs. And she can use them all to talk to people.

Koko can ask for almost anything she needs or wants. She can describe past happenings. She can ask questions. She even talks to herself. An angry Koko will say some pretty mean things to people. A happy Koko can tell jokes! And Patterson found out something else that makes Koko seem human. Once in a while, the gorilla will tell lies.

One day Koko broke the kitchen sink in her house trailer. Penny asked Koko why she broke the sink. Koko signed back that *she* wasn't the one who broke it. It was someone else, she signed. It was Kate, one of her human trainers!

Though Koko is still learning, she has also started to teach other gorillas to use sign language. In 1976 she was joined by a five-and-a-half-year-old gorilla named Mike. Koko helps the trainers by practicing with Mike. She drills him on her two favorite signs, "Koko" and "tickle." Koko loves to be tickled. But even with

person
talk
GSmith

Koko's tutoring, Mike still has much to learn. He knows only about 35 signs. And he doesn't sign fast enough to please the strictest of all his teachers, Koko.

The fact that Koko seems able to teach Mike gives animal scientists a lot of hope for their future work. Perhaps human sign language may become a natural way for apes to communicate with one another and with their human neighbors. Researchers are now trying to find out if sign language can be passed down from adult apes to their young.

Chapter 4

A Closer Look at Dolphin Talk

As we have already seen, animals don't need a human sign language or human teachers to be able to "talk" with each other. They have been communicating since the beginning of life on earth. Scientists are only now starting to understand how their languages work.

We know that dolphins seem to be able to tell each other when there is trouble in the ocean. These sea animals seem to be able to warn one another. And once a warning has been given, dolphins can help each other out. This is very important for mother dolphins while they are raising their young.

When a dolphin is born far below the surface of the ocean, it does not know how to swim. But the dolphin

A mother dolphin can get help in caring for her baby by sending out a special signal to other grown-up dolphins.

is a mammal. It needs air to breathe. Somehow the young dolphin must reach the water's surface even before it has learned to swim up from the ocean floor. The mother dolphin can't lift the baby to the surface alone. It is too small and too slippery to stay on the mother's back or to be pushed by her nose. What does the mother do? She "phones" for help!

The dolphin's way of calling for help may be even better than any telephone people use. She uses a series of double whistles. The first whistle is loud and becomes louder. The second whistle is loud but gets softer. Within seconds her whistled "phone call" is answered by another female dolphin. The two adults move together, dive under the baby, and catch it on their backs.

Carried quickly to the surface of the ocean, the young dolphin reaches up above the water for its first gulps of air. From then on, the baby will need to surface every six minutes to breathe. As long as it is unable to do this alone — for the next few days or even weeks — it must be helped by the two adult dolphins. And all the while, the two whistle softly at the young dolphin in a special "baby talk," teaching it to take care of itself.

Dolphins also have ways of handling danger. Take the case of a young dolphin being chased by a great white shark. As the youngster leaps and plunges to avoid the shark's fierce jaws, it makes sharp clicking sounds. These clicks are a dolphin distress call — a kind of secret SOS. In only a moment the call is answered. A dolphin "rescue team" rushes in to save their young friend.

When a dolphin is hurt, the distress call lets other dolphins know exactly where their injured friend is.

The dolphin's secret SOS can bring other dolphins to the rescue. These friendly sea mammals have been known to save the lives of human swimmers as well.

But to the dolphins' enemies, like the great white shark, the distress signals don't give away a thing. Only dolphins understand the special call.

Scientists have been studying the mysteries of dolphin communication for years. They are no longer surprised by the dolphin's high intelligence. But there is much they still don't understand about the language of this friendly animal of the sea.

The afternoon show at Florida's Seaquarium has just ended. A group of visitors has crowded around the edge of the dolphin pool. Everyone wants to get a closer look at the stars of the show — two dolphins called Orano and Magar. Their trainer stands on a platform over the pool. Shading her eyes, she looks toward Magar and Orano splashing about at the other end of the tank. Suddenly the trainer whistles. Her whistle seems to be a signal the dolphins know very well. They race across the pool at a speed of more than 25 knots (26.9 miles per hour; 43.3 kilometers per hour).

There is a good reason for Magar and Orano to be swimming so fast. To the dolphins this whistle means, "Come and get it!" The trainer takes some fish from a bucket and tosses them to the two dolphins. Leaping high in the air, Magar and Orano catch the fish in their open mouths. Then they plunge to the bottom of the tank, turn a few somersaults, and climb right back to the surface again. They break through the water and leap more than 20 feet (6.1 meters), their high-pitched squeaking sounds filling the air.

"You're welcome!" shouts the dolphins' trainer. She claps her hands once, and the dolphins race up to the pool's edge. The visitors lean over the rail for a closer look at Magar and Orano.

Suddenly there is water flying everywhere. The dolphins have dived and returned to spray water over everyone around the pool. The shower has come as they empty the air in their lungs through holes at the tops of their heads. They are called *blowholes.* Through these openings the dolphins take in fresh air and let out the air they have used for breathing while they were under the water.

"Sorry," says the dolphins' trainer to the soaking wet crowd of people around the pool. "That's just one of their practical jokes. But a dolphin's blowhole is used for more than just playing tricks. You've heard all the different kinds of sounds that Magar and Orano make. You may not have known it, but they use these sounds to 'talk' to each other."

The visitors at Seaquarium have just seen how dolphins can force air through the blowhole to make a

MI
QUARIUM

water shower. Dolphins can also force air through the blowhole to make sounds. It works something like a steam whistle. Some scientists think this is how dolphins talk with one another.

Inside the dolphin's throat there are soft skin folds. These folds of skin can make air vibrate through the blowhole. The vibrating air produces different kinds of sounds. It may seem as though dolphins talk through their mouths the way humans do. Their mouths do seem to move when they make sounds. But they do not make sounds the way we do at all.

Many scientists now believe that there is a dolphin language. But it doesn't have words. Instead, it is made up of *tones* — like the different sounds or *pitches* of musical notes. Each tone, or separate sound, has a meaning that all dolphins understand. Scientists have already discovered six different tones in the dolphin's whistle — *A, B, C, D, E,* and *F* — just like the notes, or keys, on a piano keyboard.

These tones aren't really the same as words. They express a mood — or feeling. For example, our voices sound one way when we are in a happy mood and have another sound or tone when we feel sad. Our tone of voice can help show how we feel, or what kind of mood we are in.

The dolphin and the whale are mammals. Both need air to breathe. There is a small piece of muscle just inside the blowhole. This is an opening at the top of the animal's head that lets air in and out of its lungs. The muscle's movement helps the animal make different kinds of sounds as air escapes through the blowhole.

In dolphin "talk," tone *A* is a greeting, like "Hello!" or "How are you?" Tones *B* and *D* tell whether the dolphin is male or female. *C*, *E*, and *F* are like the tones of voice people might use when talking. The tones dolphins use depend on the mood of the "conversation": sad, happy, tired, excited, and so on.

All the dolphin's sounds, along with the way it moves and the tones it uses, tell something about the dolphin's mood. A trainer can tell if a dolphin is happy, afraid, excited, curious, teasing, hurt, or comfortable by the sounds it makes. Today we know that there are about 60 groups of dolphin sounds much like human sentences. And the dolphin's language does not seem to be a simple one at all. Some scientists even think the dolphin language may have a larger vocabulary than human languages.

A Final Word

It is exciting to learn that humans are standing at the edge of a whole new field of science — the science of animal language. Some of us are already "talking" with animals that cannot speak as we do. But why should we *want* to talk to dolphins or apes — or, for that matter, to field mice or elephants?

Scientists still have much to learn about how the human brain works. Scientists who study language want to know if there is a part of the brain that controls our ability to speak, read, and write.

These scientists are especially interested in animal language. Do animals have languages of their own? Can these animals learn whole new languages? If so, maybe there is some center in all well-developed brains that controls the ability to use language. But exactly what is this center? And *where* is it? If scientists can learn how the brain controls language, then they can help people who have trouble learning to speak, write, and read.

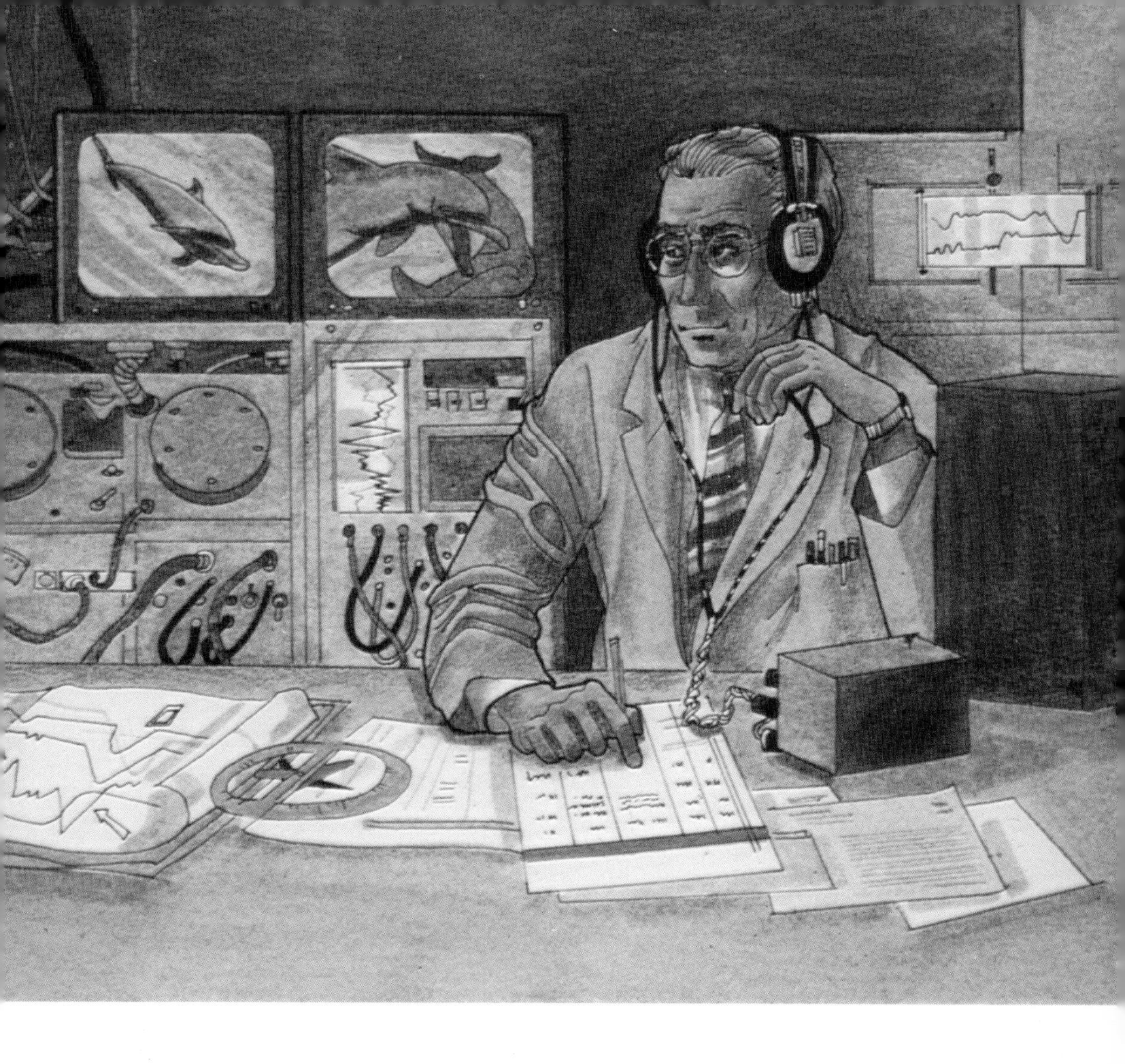

Animals like dolphins and apes may help us solve the millions of mysteries still inside our own heads — the mysteries of the human brain. What is more, these animals may even help us understand mysteries far beyond our own earth!

Sooner or later, it is possible that astronauts will meet living creatures on some unknown planet. These life forms probably will not have a language we can understand. How will humans talk with the unknown beings? Maybe the best way to start is by learning to communicate with the nonhuman creatures on our *own* planet. After all, the more we know about animal language, the more practice we'll have in making friendly contact with beings many light-years away from us in space.

But most scientists are "talking" with animals to find information they can use much closer to home. They expect to solve some mysteries that have puzzled people since the beginning of history. And as we make sense of these strange puzzles, we are almost certain to learn many new things about the strangest animals of all — *ourselves*!